NOBODY'S DAUGHTER

Katie Reilly

SLOW...please Press
Marblehead, Massachusetts

Copyright © 1997 Katie Reilly

Published by:

⟨SLOW⟩
please!

SLOW...please Press
Marblehead, Massachusetts

All rights reserved. No part of this publication may be reproduced or transmitted in any form or by any means, electronic or mechanical, including photocopy, recording, or any information storage or retrieval system, without the express written permission of the publisher.

Editor:	Barbara Wolf, First Person Press
Production Coordinator:	Nancy L. Sarles, NSarles & Associates
Book and Jacket Design:	Lori Lynn Hoffer, Lori Hoffer Graphics
Author Photograph:	Andrew Swaine Studios, Salem, MA
Cover Photograph:	Matthew Nutting
'Living Daisy' Illustration:	Colleen Reilly, "from one grows another"

**Library of Congress Cataloging
Card Number: 96-071980**

Reilly, Katie
Nobody's Daughter
ISBN 0-9656367-04

Address all inquiries to:
SLOW...please Press
P. O. Box 4000
Marblehead, MA 01945

NOBODY'S DAUGHTER

My heart reaches out with indescribable gratitude
to our three phenomenal children:

To Bill for his deep voice of insistence
To Colleen for her gentle whispers and hugs
To Mike for his clear-cut and spirited enthusiasm

You kept reminding me to "follow my dream"
and at times you were more devoted to that dream
than was I. Now my first book is done . . .
please know that you are part of
each page . . . I do adore you,

Mom, Kate, The Slowlady

*Dedicated to
my extraordinary mother,*

Dorothy Theresa Hayes Buckley

*For teaching me the gentle joys of Life -
birthday cakes of sand with seaweed candles
and countless, everyday joys that others seldom notice.*

I shall always carry you within me.

PROLOGUE

Dear Mom,
You are gone.
No one is here to console me,
To hug me,
To let me be weak,
To let me sob for hours
And remind me,
As you would have,
That tears are the first step
To strength and growth.

If only you were here,
If only you had left me a note,
"Kateso, don't forget to cry."
But I did forget.
I cried for everyone but for myself,
As if I were not worth the tears.

I was on my own,
Only Dad was here,
And, as always,
His message was so powerful:
"Crying is for babies,"
"Crying will get you nowhere."
I felt I had no choice
But to remain strong.

For years I grieved on paper,
Silently,
So I would burden no one.
But when Dad died,
I knew I had mourned with him
For his loss,

But never for my own.
The journey to this point
Has been heartwrenching.
Many times, so many times,
My energies
Became fragmented.
Overburdened,
I doubted I could reach
My destination.

Yet, I know now,
I can go on without you,
I really can,
And I know
I am carrying with me
The best of what you were.
I know now,
I can rejoice in your life
And celebrate my own
In a new-found way.

For years I dreaded this goodbye.
I regret that I can only say it on paper.
But it is time for me to move on,
My dearest mother,
It is truly time
To lay you to rest.

Love always,

Kateso

Your Kateso

A gray-haired doctor
Walked up to me
With that telling question:
"Are you Mrs. Buckley's daughter?"
"Yes," I said.
"Is anyone else here?"
"No, just me,
But I can call them."

Without hesitation,
Without taking me somewhere private,
"Your mom has cancer.
She has fluid around her heart.
That's why she can't breathe.
She has a short time to live."

I grabbed his arm.
Without thinking,
I put my hand on his face.
"I'm sorry, doctor,
I just have to make sure
This is real."

"I thought she had pleurisy," I pleaded.
"I just told you,
She has cancer.
You'd better call family members,
Some decisions need to be made."

I questioned him again,
"Are you sure it's not pleurisy?"
He turned and walked away.

I remember
The smell of the hospital
Hit me
Like a Mack truck.
You know, that hospital smell.
I remember everyone in white
Rushing
As I stood
Invisible.

The vigil begins.
I know the goal,
That she never realize
She's going to die.
Never.

So I dress as a clown,
I dress in johnnies,
One day I drape surgical masks
All over me,
On my head, arms, legs, face and breasts.
I need to make her laugh.
To lessen her fear,
Her fright,
And the hysteria inside her
That she tries so hard to contain.

I try to distract her
From all that is happening,
The monitors beeping, the morphine dripping,
IVs, blood tests, pills and shots.
I need to make her laugh,
As she has done for me
So many times.
And when I become ridiculous,
She pretends she's embarrassed,
But I know she is not.
She loves all that I do.

My God,
She knows me so well.
She also must know
She's dying.

Dichotomy,
The most indefinite pronouncement of our lives,
Yet, we respond with decisive fervor
That is immediate,
Blatant.
We are clicking,
We are precise,
We are on time.
We are on a schedule
Unlike any we have experienced
Nine-to-five.
We are soldiers,
Marching with an undeniable patriotism.
Harm to ourselves does not matter,
As long as the harm does not deter our cause.
She is our cause.
Every waking minute,
She is our cause.
We feel as good and as bad as she,
But we feel nothing for ourselves
Except, at times,
I begrudgingly acknowledge fatigue
And squelch my desperate and unruly panic.

Only now
Do I realize
How much we put aside
So we could handle
What we had to do,
To watch her die.

There is not
One morning
I do not arise
And yearn to hear
The pounding of the keys.
The pounding
Has become my constant reminder
That I am in control
And
I can be strong. . .
I must be strong.

My husband leaves early each day
For the hospital
To feed her yogurt or toast or jello
Before he goes to work.
He is the son
She never had.
And no son
Could ever be
More gentle,
More loving,
More tender.

I arrive later
And so often
I find his notes.
(God, I wish I had kept them.)
"Dot, I didn't want to wake you,
You were sleeping so sound.
I'll be back tonight.
See you then.

Love,
Your Bill."

Leaving Camelot
En route
To hell on earth,
I depart
A cocoon of brilliant colors,
Mellow gulls, dancing jack rabbits,
And children's summer laughter
To arrive
At bleak corridors
Of groaning and suffering
And plain and sterile white.
Oh, my God,
My Mom's dying!

Her keenness and perception are undaunted.
Oh, to hear her actually laugh today,
She's Dottie again,
And I swear for a minute
I forgot what she had!

She wants everyone at work,
Me with my kids,
Joan not to drive,
Buck to eat and rest.
She is always concerned
So much more
With our needs
Than hers.

The sadness I feel tonight
Is unlike anything in the past eight days.
I saw Mom comfortable,
Hopeful,
Sitting up and eating.
She even laughed.
She talked of feeling good,
Of trying to walk to the door for me.

Tonight she is out of pain and anguish,
And I want her home with me.
Before, I wanted her out of her suffering,
And by far,
I found it less difficult
To let her go.
But now she is my Mom again,
Witty, intuitive,
Loving me more than herself.
The thought
Of not having her forever
is unbearable.

My happiness revolves around loving her.
I need to love her!
There is no other way
For me to be happy.
And I love
The way she adores me!

This enigma called death
Is becoming too familiar,
As are doctors, nurses,
Unsightly hospital corridors,
And the antiseptic smell
Of sheets and spreads.
Thank God we retain the trite sentiments
So important to Buckleys:
Her pocket Bible placed in the drawer,
Her scapula pinned to the mattress,
Her beads resting on the nightstand.
Her two favorite quilts from home
Always within reach
To comfort her during fearful nights.
These are Mom's steadfast hold,
Her link,
Her will
To go home.

And, while she cannot be
In her own cribby bed,
Her quilts make her feel that she is.
I am sure she can feel Buck's toes
When she rubs her feet
On the wool.
I am so sure
Remembering
The familiar
Gives my mom
Incorrigible strength
To live on!

"If only"
I've heard her say that so often.
But "if onlys"
Have become wishful thinking
Instead of attainable goals.
"I know I could get better
If only
They'd just let me
Go home," she sighs.

On Swimming in the ocean each day. . .

I've begun swimming every day
Since Mom became ill,
As if to numb my body and soul.

The cold water of the morning
Numbs yesterday's hurts
And gives me renewed strength
To endure
Today's pain.

Never before
Have the happiest things in my life
Been the saddest.
The weather has been consistently beautiful,
The flowers in our garden
Are drying out after the spring rains.
It's a northeast sparkler,
The geraniums are brilliant for once,
(Mom and I kill geraniums!)
And when my five-year-old
Swam the width of the pool today,
She exclaimed
"Wait till Dottie sees me!"
Never have I felt such pain
From such joy.

My sadness has increased
From daily
To hourly
To the minute.
I can no longer predict its arrival.
I only long for my mother
To share this day of beauty
Here by the sea.

Call it what you want:
Courage,
Guts,
Determination,
Perseverance,
Love of life,
Whatever,
My mom has it.
Never has any war
Seen such a victory,
Nor any soldier waged
A more tedious battle.

They said she would never come home,
They said she would never walk,
That she would never be better,
But she's fooled them all
And their medical degrees.
She's coming home,
She's walked,
She's gained weight!

So we've decorated every telephone pole en route
With home-made posters and yellow balloons.
Signs on the doors, front and back,
"Welcome Home, Dottie,
This is where you belong!"
"Dottie's home! Yippee!"
And we'll celebrate
Her coming home to us
The way she promised she would.

If only for a while.

I sit by
While Mom sleeps,
And for me
There is comfort
In knowing
She is not feeling the headache
Or the needles
Or the worry.

My God, thank you for this time,
This precious quiet time with her.
But now, dear God,
Please teach me
To want much less.

It is so haunting
Standing here,
Outside my mother's hospital room,
Talking behind her back
About when she will die,
Asking her doctor,
"When do you think
It will happen."

IT always IT.
Never mention the word.
I really know nothing about It.
I hear it,
Read it,
Write it,
And even sometimes
I catch myself saying it,
But God knows I know nothing about It.

IT happens fast,
Even when you have five months warning,
But it will take me days,
Weeks, months and years
To understand IT,
Comprehend IT,
Deal with IT,
Submit to IT,
Accept IT.

Her zest and enthusiasm
Is unlike anyone's.
Everyone loves to hear her hearty laugh,
Her happy screams,
Her hellish swears.
She makes us feel so alive!

Thus, even now,
Near the end,
I demand that of her.

When the phone rang,
Bill answered in the kitchen,
And he called me downstairs.

"Your Mom just died."

He may have said the time,
I don't remember.
I dropped to my knees,
Put my head on the floor,
And gasped.
He grabbed my shoulders and hugged me.
I wanted to scream,
But caught myself
So the kids would not hear.

I stopped crying.
I had to get to the hospital
To my Dad,
To my sisters,
And,
To my Mom.

She's gone.

November 22, 1983

I can't bear the feel of a hug
Or a kiss
Without crying.
My home brings pain
That I never expected.
The photos, collages, cards,
And memorabilia
Tear at my heart.
I want to sell the house,
To move to a place less beautiful,
Where I have not enjoyed
The joyous seasons with my mother.
I want to walk a lawn and sit in a chair,
Where she has never been.
I cannot bear the pain,
I want the pansies and marigolds
To die.
I want the green and yellow painted another color.
My home can never be as happy again.
God, please help me!

They say my Mom has died.
Those words mean nothing to me;
Perhaps it is truer
To say I have died.
For all the life in me seems to have left
My body
And my spirit.
All the zest and vigor
That was once mine
Has disappeared;
And I am not sure if the departure
Was sudden
Or gradual.
All I know is that the life in me has gone
And the effort to function —
Or to merely stay awake —
Is insurmountable for me.

Who will come with me this year
To welcome the first tulips,
To watch for them
And thank me once again
For planting the bulbs around the house.

Who will help me greet
The first southwest wind
And predict the barometer
For the spring and summer.

Who will want to be with me
During those warm days of doing nothing together.
How will I ever greet
This first spring of my life
Without her smile,
Her Kateso,
Her voice,
Her laugh,
Her jaunts.
Her face coming through my kitchen door.

I see her walking the yard.
I hear her voice
With the kids in the playroom.
I hear her raving
Of how warm and happy my house is.
Did she not see herself in every room
As I did so often?
Her spirit lived here with us.
Did she not know that?

I walk in
To what is now
Dad's house
This first time;
And I try
To make as much noise
And commotion as possible,
As if I can disguise
The silence,
The emptiness,
The awkwardness,
The obviousness
Of what is missing.
Mom's boisterous,
Outrageous,
Demonstrative
Greeting.

Dad,
You walk down my driveway
And, for the very first time,
She is not with you.
It's become final.
She will not
Walk down that path with you again,
Nor in my door
Or on our beaches.
Never will her laughter
Adorn my shore.

Dad,
You sit and eat without her beside you.
She isn't there to interrupt you,
To "Oh, Buck" you,
Those days will be no more.

Dad,
You walk away,
Down my long driveway,
You are alone
Like never before.
It becomes so final,
The realization
Is
She will never
Be with you again.

Hey, God:
I know how many are residing at your house.
Are you sure you're loving her enough?
She loves being loved, you know!

At this time of my life,
I have no time for triteness
Or the picayune.
There is an intensity to each day,
Each hour,
Sometimes even to the minute,
An intensity I have experienced only once before,
Ironically, after giving birth.

I need to be purposeful and sincere,
To be honest,
To be selective
With hugs and kisses
And how I spend
My time and my energy.

Of all the times when
I cannot compromise on a hug,
A hello,
A thank you
Or a phone call . . .
Dear God, it is now.

Please, dear God, I beg of you,
Spare me all the shams of life
Until I am again strong,
Strong enough to laugh at them once again
And not permit them to bring out all the anger in me,
Because they rob me of what I need now. . .
Quiet,
Honesty,
And a human heart that cares.
Never did I dream I could be asking for so much
By asking for so little - another lesson bitterly learned.
Please do not be shallow with me, World,
For I have not the tolerance for even you.
Later,
But,
Please,
Not now.

I can no longer reach my Mom
To make me feel whole
At the times
When I feel most like coming apart;
This is a new challenge for me,
To be whole without her,
A mystery not easily solved.

The prolonged darkness
Has been such a comfort to me this winter.
I've loved it grey and dismal,
I've thrived
On the fog and drizzle and mud.
I have not missed the sight of flowers
Or the sounds of birds.

The outside has coincided so very nicely
With my aching heart.
The bleakness of the season
Has made my emptiness feel less obvious
In contrast to the coming spring.

Dear God,
Be my friend once again,
And let the winter
Last a bit longer this year.

I have tried very hard
To cry,
I really have.
But the tears won't surface.
They aren't free.
They are silent and trapped.
After all,
They have grown quite accustomed
To not showing themselves,
For, even as a child,
My writing was always encouraged,
But never my tears.

There have been so many sunny days
That I've stopped thinking about the rainy ones
And never gave a second thought to the fog.
Why should I not wear a raincoat
Like so many others?
Why should I become accustomed to sunglasses
Instead of an umbrella?

My mom provided me with such joy,
I thought that clear and sunny weather
Would last each season of my life.

I do dread the spring.
I am so petrified - so totally frightened -
That if I do not begin to miss her less
During the cold of winter,
I shall never recover
From the first spring of my life
Without her.
I need her so in the Spring,
Or I shall never be the same!
God, please help me now!

As bad as death is,
The scars of dying
Are more painful and burdensome.
Reliving all those days,
Those weeks,
Those months.
Her face,
Her voice,
Her tears.
Thinking of her
Usurps all my energies.

The beauty of the summer was my enemy,
A source of pain - not joy.
How soothing it is to feel the cold chill
Of Fall's north wind,
To have the days rightfully shorter,
To see dark at six a.m.
And not a glistening sunrise,
With flowers abloom and birds chirping.
It is easier
But so much lonelier
To deal with grief this Fall,
For the seasons of my life have changed forever.

I ever-so-closely watch
My Dad.
He performs like a soldier,
His clean-shaven face,
Plaid pants,
Cashmere sweater,
As if the familiar will bring her back.

The saddest moment
Is Dad
Bending a limb of the Christmas tree,
Holding onto it with one hand,
With the other reaching for a bulb.

The process is painful to watch.
He is alone,
Surrounded by all of us,
His sons-in-law and daughters,
He is still alone.
So much more alone
Than any of us.
He is one,

Alone,
By himself.

If it is true
That there is a heaven
And that in fact,
Her spirit lives,
Is it also true and final
That my spirit is dead?

When will the lightness return,
The laughter,
The silliness,
Without the tears
Following?
How long will it be
Before Kateso
Appears again?

Hi God,

You must be surprised to hear from me
After all this time,
But I had so many unanswered questions to resolve
Finally, I am convinced
She is happier with you,
That her leaving is for the best,
But adjusting to everyday life
Without her
Has been so hard.

That's actually why I am writing to you.
I know it's Sunday
And you must be so busy,
But I was thinking that perhaps,
Before the day's chores and prayers begin,
You might spare her for an earthly minute
Or even half a second.

I need her so today,
Like never before.
Lord, if I could just capture a glimpse of her,
Even from the back.
Maybe she could wear those blue slacks
And the hot pink blazer she loved.
Just three or four steps
Would warm my heart,
And I promise,
I wouldn't ask
For more than that.

Or perhaps I could just hear her voice today.
Just a word, not a conversation,
Just a word would be all.
Perhaps she could just utter my name,
"Kateso"
She used to say it
Like no one else.

Never has a human being felt
With me
And for me
As she.
So deeply,
So desperately.
Any happiness that was hers,
She would relinquish to me;
Any sadness that was mine,
She would gladly inherit.
Who else
Will ever love me this way?

Some days I am strong enough
To handle the world.
Other days, I am not;
And I feel the need
To be wrapped neatly
In a box
Clearly marked
"Fragile,"
"Handle With Care."

I miss her
Unrestricted love for me.
I miss her physical affection.
I miss the way
She made me feel
When I was with her,
Full
And real,
Loved
And adored.

I shall always cling to these memories,
For these memories will forever remind me
Of a time,
A feeling,
A stage,
A fanciful way of life.
They will always remind me of
My mother's love.

My way of life,
Oh to have it as it was.
It will never be that way again.

What a fanciful life I devoured
Of fun-filled, sparkling days
On the sea and the snow,
Carefree shopping, conversing,
And being with my best friend.

What an intrusion — That goddamn disease!
To rob us of her.
I am so glad we wandered together,
To thrift shops and sandy shores.
I am so glad we giggled together
And laughed about nothing,
For those days will be no more.

I am so glad she knew my children
And loved my husband
More than any note of hers could describe.
No one who saw their devotion
Will ever forget it;
It will be no more.

I am glad we shared some common pains,
For only the knowing of helping her
Will help me now
Not to miss her so.

Today is hard.
I cannot believe that today
I cannot talk to her on the phone,
Laugh with her,
Kiss her once more
Or touch her for a fleeting second.
These have become my dreams,
My wishes.
They will be no more.

I keep typing;
I keep pounding away
At these keys.
And
How very proud I am
That I have not
Shed a tear!

A year ago,
A lifetime ago,
Something I read?
Or was it something a close friend related to me?
Not anything that happened to me first-hand.

A year ago,
A lifetime ago,
I remember it being summer.
I remember the heat
And how it ganged up on me
And drained me.

I remember at times, departing the hospital,
Knowing how a battered fighter must feel,
Trying to recoup his strengths,
By the count of ten.

I remember that deep-breathing
Became a way of life for me
And the only remedy
For finding just a bit more courage,
Just a bit more strength,
Just a bit more of whatever it was
That let me keep going,
So I was able to hold on just a bit longer,
Till I got outside,
Till I got to my car
So I could scream,
So I could cry,
So I could be hysterical.

A year ago.
It flew by
Only when there was no pain for her.
And when the pain returned,
I would once again yearn
For the time to pass quickly.

A year ago.
Only the missing
Makes this irrational mind
And empty heart
Crave that horrible year back once again.

I used to blame the coming of spring,
Then the heat of the summer,
And all the remembering of that season.
Then I blamed the smell of Fall,
The changing leaves,
The shifting wind,
The crisp air,
The smell of beef stew.
But now it's the cold of winter,
It's never felt so cold
My senses are in pain
And crave numbing.

She was our teacher,
Our master teacher.
It was she who taught us
To be strong enough to cry,
Strong enough to feel,
Honest enough to expose our feelings.
It was she
Who brought advice to each crisis
And compassion to our personal sorrows.

It was she who lived each day for us
And not for herself.
This was her gift.
Thus, none of us who knew her —
Will ever be
Ordinary again.

I am trying to concentrate
On what actually is,
Rather than what was,
Or what might have been.

How she would love
To see my children swim,
To watch their strokes
Become strong
And self-assured.

How thrilled and excited
She would be
To know that my children too
Adore the ocean!

You had said goodbye to everyone,
Except for me,
And for months,
And now years,
I have wondered and worried
What that might have meant.
That perhaps you loved me too much?
Or could it be,
Was it even conceivable,
That you could have loved me too little?

My eyes
Are so sore.
They have been traumatized,
For they have witnessed the harrows of death,
The joys of life,
The miracle of birth.
The extremes without warning,
Have made them tired and strained.

My eyes have tried to decipher
All the happenings
And to bring visual meaning
To an aching heart.
But the season of my year
Has blurred their vision,
For so much of the beauty of spring
Was shared with a companion
They no longer see.

Thus, there is a blank stare to my eyes.
They do not sparkle or dance with the mere thought
Of daffodils and daisies or southwest winds.
Rather, they prefer the shade this season.
They find it hard to face the sun,
For even the sun's warmth
Is no longer soothing,
But painful,
Regardless of this winter's pallor.

Holidays,
My God,
Never were there so many.
Never were they so hard to survive.
Just as I manage
To survive one
And endure the letdown,
There comes another.

In California, so I'm told,
Orchids are brought
To rest homes
During their dormant season
And returned home
Once they are again ready
To bloom.

How I do wish
That here in the East
I could find a rest home
For my aching heart,
For although it craves to feel again,
It needs only
A respite
Of pampering,
Patience
And
Unconditional
Love.

My sister Susan
Said something profound today.
"Mom was an initiator,"
Susan said.
"So often
She sensed the future for one of us.
Without revealing
That she foresaw our destinies,
She taught us to prepare."
Susan said it was only normal
That Mom should be the first to die.
And since Susan came very close to death, herself,
That held extra meaning for me.
Mom would guide us into death
As she had guided us
Into life.

I followed Dad's footsteps
To Mom's grave.
Each step of mine
Safely hidden in his.
But I knew
The day would come
When his footprints
Would no longer conceal mine.
This reminder of mortality
Chilled me
To my very bones.

He has cried so much with me,
But perhaps you did not know that.
Each holiday
Has been a struggle for him,
To withstand the exaggerated loneliness
Of being one.
He seems to rally, though,
When others appear;
But with me,
He cries.

I would have to say,
Today was the best and happiest
I have seen my dad in years.
He spent the day
With Mares, Bart
And those incredible kids.
Mares made him a roast chicken
With potatoes and vegetables.
She sat in his lap,
Hugged him and loved him
As only Mares can.
She made him feel
He belonged somewhere again.
He was becoming a grandfather
And loving it.

He camouflaged
His disease so well,
That none of us
Even knew
How thin
And frail
His body and spirit had become.
Only when I helped him
Into the tub
On that summer's day
Did I realize,
Yes,
He was dying.

My God, he's gone too.

August 1, 1987

The doors swing open.
A nurse walks toward me,
She says those words I dread,
"Are you Mr. Buckley's daughter?"
"Yes,"
And without a word
She hands me his suitcase,
My introduction to death.

My mom was the most practical,
She brought a brown bag.
My Dad brought a suitcase,
The same one he packed and unpacked
Over and over again when he came to visit
After Mom died.
I knew everything inside Mom's bag
Would be neat and orderly.
It was.
I knew everything inside Dad's
Would be in a ball.
It was.

It took me months to open that suitcase
And when I did,
I cried for hours and hours.
I sobbed and lost my breath
The way we do
When we are babies.

There have been
Oh, perhaps 500 times this weekend
When I have taken deep breaths
Or held my jaw so tightly
I thought it would crack,
Trying ever so hard
To hold back the intensity of sadness.
I am so empty.
I am grasping
At recollections of Dad a week ago
When I still had a father to visit,
To be strong for,
To brace up for,
To be loved by.

I am now a different child.
I am orphaned.
The two anchors in my life have gone,
Leaving me behind.

"Life goes on,"
"You have a lot to live for,"
"You had him for a long time,"
"He was really getting up there."
I need no pep talks, thank you,
From those who have both parents
And who have never watched,
Or even thought about
The horror
Of watching,
A loved one die.

Rage is the root
Of my sleeplessness,
Always to awaken
To being
Nobody's Daughter.

I remember
My Dad sat by himself,
Staring at the ocean,
His profile strong
And reconciled.

Without speaking a word,
I grasped
His weathered hand.
He spoke to me
In a gentle whisper
So unlike my Father:
"Katie, You're going where I've already been."
I nodded,
And neither of us spoke for hours.

In a few short weeks
He, too, was gone,
And I have clung
To that quiet moment
And those fragile words
Ever since.

Today feels like
The day after Labor Day
Or the day after a hurricane.
Dead silence,
Stillness,
So terribly, terribly empty.
Everywhere I look
I see my dad.
Sitting or walking or swimming
Or bent over
Pulling weeds from between the bricks.

I see him everywhere,
But his chair is empty.
The couch he slept on is empty,
The chaise on the hill
Is vacant.

My strength came in comforting him,
My comfort came in consoling him;
For as much as he leaned on me,
I, too, leaned on him.

Only in believing he needed me
Did I become strong.
Only in letting him be weak
Could I handle more of what had to be.
As he so often reminded me,
Life must go on.

Sometimes,
In a furor of loneliness,
I say to myself with anger,
I envy people who live far away
And only see their Mom and Dad
Every five or six years.
It is only the extreme joy I have reaped
That makes my sadness so deep,
So penetrating,
So desperate.

I swallow,
I breath deeply,
I am once again glad
I lived so close,
Physically and emotionally,
To these dear people.
They were well-worth
The pain.

I do not know
What is going on
Inside my heavy heart.
Am I anticipating the arrival of our ducks
To my door this spring,
Or is it their absence?
I do not know.

Is it the crocuses outside my kitchen
Or the thought of the bulbs I planted
With the tool my Dad presented to me with such pride.
I do not know.

Is it the longing to tell Mom and Dad
Of Tort's great raise,
Or Mary and Bart's new baby?
I do not know what this emptiness means,
For, as I gaze around me,
I see my life
Blissfully and miraculously full!

There is a need in me
To be needed
As a daughter,
Not a wife to her husband,
A mother to her child,
A sister to her sibling.
But as a daughter!

As time goes by
I am finding out
It is not the cold wind of winter,
The debilitating heat of summer,
The sweet aroma of spring,
Or the boastful blue skies of autumn.
It is everything,
Everywhere,
During every season.

I dread the smell of yellow marigolds.
The sight of red bows at Christmas,
The NYNEX ads that say, ' Hi Dad.'

I despise shopping
And catching a glimpse
Of peanut butter and jelly,
Spice drops,
And Whitman's holiday chocolates.

I cringe at the sight
Of blue ice packs in the freezer,
And extra-strength Tylenol on a shelf.

I resent false hope,
Of rallying one more time.

I cry when I see that my son
Stores the dog's tennis ball in our mailbox,
Like his grandfather.

We planted a garden last spring,
you know, my Dad and I.
He pointed to where he wanted each seedling
And I yielded to his sense of spacing.
I would have planted more
And not left so early that day
If only I had known
He would not be with me
To share their glorious colors
Only a short time later.

My life
Has gone from a full house
To emptiness,
Empty dinner tables,
Empty chairs,
Empty rooms,
Empty expressions
In my family's eyes.
When will it be full again?
Will it ever be
The way it was?

My Dad's anniversary mass
Was today.
My irrational, homesick heart
Thought for sure he'd be there
At the church to greet me,
To tap me on the head and say
"You look nice, Katie.
Your mom would like your outfit."
I would hug him,
But he would not hug me.
I would grab his arm
As we walked up the stairs.
But today,
I stood alone.

Come with me,
My poor, dear, fragile flowers,
Here I am.
I have come to rescue you from the soil
That has gone bad,
The soil that has destroyed the roots
Which gave you life,
The soil that has rotted and withered your ferns,
The same soil that once
Made you brilliant and happy.

Worry not, my fragile friends,
I'll take you home with me,
To shelter and pamper you.
I promise,
You will thrive,
You will be brilliant again,
The way you were
When Dad was here
To care for you.

Mom and Dad's house,
Is to be sold.
The flowers we had planted
Were uncared for.
I removed each wretched plant
As gingerly as I had handled my newborns.
I dug each one,
And my sister stared at me.
She had never seen me so irrational,
Nor had I.

Uprooting each flower,
I cried.
My roots were being destroyed.
Now, to return home,
To plant,
To give birth again.

I dug and planted
All the next day . . .
The flowers are thriving,
And given time,
So shall I.

I spied a crow at my window today.
Mr. Crow, ya know
I used to feel so special.
I could pick up the phone
Or hop in my car
Any day of the week
And relish a hug from someone
Who truly adored me.
My parents' love was more forgiving
Than anyones'.

Big black crow,
Do me a favor,
Bring this message to my folks.
Tell them I'm doing all right
And not to worry.
I'm fine,
But tell them
I miss them so.

You did not say goodbye,
Nor did I;
And only now do I understand
That neither of us could bare
The pain of leaving each other
Or of hearing that word
Uttered out loud.

I woke this morning
To the sound of wailing gulls,
Those gulls you loved to watch
At the bank's edge.
They were crying for you.
They knew you had gone
And taken Mom with you,
Along with my place of refuge and shelter.
They knew when you left,
There would not be anyone with whom to speak
About her gait,
Her laugh,
Her smile.
No one else to grieve with,
To despair with,
About that deepening hole
In my very human heart.

Now I realize
I grieved with you
And for you,
But never
Did I
Grieve
For myself.
The time has come
To feel the pain
I have dreaded.

It is time
For me to cry.

We women put so many
Hurts and tears aside,
And,
With the best intentions
We promise ourselves a good cry
When there is time.

The days pass into weeks,
The weeks into months,
The months into years.
We stuff our hurts and our pain,
Like a teen packing for vacation.

It is when we learn to love ourselves,
To hug ourselves
And caress our wounded hearts,
That we realize
We are well-worth the tears,
And the teardrops do come.

We must reassure our tears,
Convince them they are safe
To show themselves,
That they are worthy,
That they are loved
And that we as human beings,
We do deserve to cry.

My frail heart
Has adapted
To the unfinished feeling
That Death has left with me.

There was so much
To figure out.
How was I to know
What I should cling to
Or let go of,
Forget or remember?
I was merely a child
Without a teacher.

The journey has been long,
There has been no land
In sight.
But, alas,
I spy a beacon,
A flicker of hope
And, with a sigh,
I am reminded
Of my destination.

Oh, to be alone,
Completely and totally alone,
To hear
Only the chattering of the birds,
Anxious to play again
After their night apart.

Oh, to be alone,
So completely and totally alone,
To listen only to the trickling
Of a gentle stream
That loses itself
In a giant lake,
Never to be as fresh, as sparkling,
As independently brilliant on its own.

Oh, to be alone,
So completely and totally alone,
To understand
Every thought,
Every feeling
Every natural instinct.
My thoughts are outspoken;
They are clear and enlightened!
They are as alive
As I!

Spring is blooming
And never did I dream
This new season could be
So Brilliant,
So Vibrant,
Without her here
To share with me.

The tears on these pages,
I want to relish them,
To rejoice in their moisture.
For it is only in remembering
That I recognize
How far I have come
And how very happy
I now am.

I thought I had lost.
Then I realized
How very much I had gained.
I thought I was less.
Then I realized
I was so much more.
I thought life
Would never be as full,
And it is not.
But the emptiness
I carry with me
Day to day
Transforms into strength.

I awoke
Early this morning
And watched
As a single blade of grass
Became warmed
By the sun.

I listened
To a cricket whisper
Good morning
To a new day.

Thank you, dear God,
For a day of sunshine,
Of warm breezes
And a compliment of friends.

Thank you for giving me
A sense of self,
Of accomplishment,
Of renewed
Self-esteem.

Thank you
For the feeling of spring,
Of new hope,
Of spontaneity,
Of new-found energy,
Of rebirth.

Your body
Departed,
But your spirit remains.
More than
The image of myself,
More than the reflection
Of only one,
Your energy,
Your force,
Your love
Continues and abounds
In our three children.
Their love of the ocean,
Their love of reading,
Their love of writing,
Their love of laughter.
Your love is alive in all of us.

I see you,
I feel you,
I can smell you.
I see so much of you
In the mirror.
I see you there,
As I love my children,
As I comfort my husband,
As I worry into the early hours,
You are with me.
You are always by my side.

I am here at your grave
To speak with you
In my new voice.
I left here
Very much a tortured child;
I return here today
A woman reborn.

The happiness
I feel
Reinforces
What my tears have taught.
Not that I love you any less;
It is that I
Love myself
More!

I took a walk by myself today.
To my neighbors and my children
It was merely a stroll.
To me,
A declaration,
A Commitment,
Each step determined
And defined.

You might say
I went on a march today,
Not an amble.
Clearly,
Taking a giant step,
Resigning myself to life's finality
And to my desire
To not only survive
But to succeed!

I took a walk by myself today.
It was a celebration,
A milestone.
My oneness was exaggerated
By the determination of my stride.

I embarked on a pilgrimage today,
And my pace hastened
With the thought
Of being whole again.

I went for a walk in sunshine today,
And as I approached my kitchen door,
Joyfully rejuvenated and relieved,
The knob turned more easily
Than it had before.

I saw the ducks walking on the lawn,
And I did not burst into tears.
I was not overwhelmed.
I ran to get the bread.

Standing at the edge of the ocean,
Each breath I took was like a first.
I tore the bread into small pieces,
"Yes, I was gone for a while,
But I'm back,
And I'm never going away again."

The sky remains a vibrant blue,
September blue before its time,
Nature's way of reminding us
Of the seasons of our lives.

No matter what our grief,
Fall will follow summer's warmth;
And winter's north winds will chill our souls
But not our spirits.
Life continues,
And
We go on.

ACKNOWLEDGEMENT

I have so many people to thank . . .

Thank you to my children, for inspiring me, encouraging me and believing in me. Thank you to my husband, for encouraging me and for tolerating reams of paper in every room for so many years. Thank you to my five sisters, for loving my Mom and Dad. Thank you to Willa, for her unending love, taking care of my parents and all of us. Thank you to Uncle Bobby, for being her faithful and devoted-brother. Thank you to Peg, for being her dear, dear friend. Thank you to Buck for marrying her. Thank you to Margo and Marjorie, for retrieving all the fragments of my heart, transcribing them, and making sense of all the pain. Thank you to my fingers, for showing me the way.

About

<SLOW please!>

SLOW...please Press
Marblehead, Massachusetts

In 1987 Katie Reilly, a professed speedaholic, was rushing in her car to meet her daughter at a specific time, a specific place. When she arrived in her hurried state, she found a young girl resembling her daughter who had been struck and dragged 97 feet by a truck. Traumatized by this moment, she returned to the street the next day holding a homemade SLOW sign. In the weeks to come, she realized that it was not the SLOW sign that had made an impression on passers-by, but it was her personal plea, 'please.' And from that moment an idea was born entitled *SLOW...please!!!**

What was initiated as a public safety campaign has now evolved into a unique, nationally-recognized quality-of-life program advocating a slower pace, not just in our driving but in our daily lives. The catalyst of the campaign has been to place the very personal word *please* in all the unexpected places throughout our day – on our street signs, our trash barrels, our tee-shirts, on our automobile dashboards, our storefronts and our shaving mirrors. As founder Kate Reilly concedes, "We treat the symptoms of fast pace with a gentle reminder of Life – the word 'please' – *SLOW...Please!!!*" And it has worked!

Now ten years later as we rush our way towards the 21st century, *SLOW...please* Press shall bring that same reminder to care in the form of written prose. Our publications shall celebrate all the wonders of being a human being, while we take the time to laugh, to cry, to feel . . . while we take the time to say 'please'.

For more information on *SLOW...Please*, please write us at P.O. Box 4000, Marblehead, MA, 01945.

**SLOW...Please!!!, Inc.* is a non-profit, tax-deductible charitable institution.